Covered Bridges of Virginia and West Virginia

Copyright Statement

Covered Bridges of Virginia and West Virginia
A Guide for Photographers and Explorers

Published by Harold Stiver
Copyright 2013 Harold Stiver

Version 1.0

Table of Contents

Photo Credits

How to use this Book

For each of the 25 historical or Traditional Covered Bridges remaining in Virginia and West Virginia, we have included photographs as well as descriptive and statistical data. Traditional Covered Bridges are those that follow the building practices of the Nineteenth Century and the early part of the Twentieth Century or those built later that follow those methods. All of these bridges have had repairs done as portions wear out, and some may have been almost entirely replaced through the years. I have used "The National Society for the Preservation of Covered Bridges, Inc." list of what they consider as Traditional Bridges.

Following is data included for each bridge

Name: This is listed in bold type, and where there are other names, it is the common name or the name listed on an accompanying plaque.

Other Names: Underneath the Common Name in brackets, you will find other names that the bridge has been known by.

Nearest Township and **County** are listed.

It is frustrating to go on an excursion to see something and not be able to find it. This book offers you multiple ways to ensure that doesn't happen.

GPS Position: This is our recommended method. Enter the coordinates in a good GPS unit and it should take you right there. You, of course, must use care that you are not led off road or on a dangerous route.

Detailed Driving Directions: Directions from a town near to the bridge.

Builder: If known, the name of the original builder(s) is listed.

Year Built: As well as the year built, if it has been moved it will shown with the year preceded by the letter M and, if a major repair has been done, the year will be shown preceded by the letter R.

Truss Type: The type for the particular bridge will be listed. If you are interested in more information on the various types of trusses, access "Truss Types" from the Table of Contents.

Dimensions: The length and number of spans.

Photo Tips: The compass orientation is given which gives the user some indication of the sun position. if there are superior setup positions or other compositional elements, they may be noted. You may also find some useful ideas from reading "Photographing Covered Bridges" from the Table of Contents.

Notes: A place where you can find additional items of interest about the bridge.

World Index Number:
Covered bridges are assigned a number to keep track of them which consists of three numbers separated by hyphens.

The first number represents the number of the U.S. State in alphabetical order. Following number 50 for the 50th state are additional numbers for Canadian provinces. Thus the numbers 05 represents California.

The second set of numbers represents the county of that state, again based on alphabetical order. Humboldt is the 12th county alphabetically in California, and it is designated as 05-12.

Each bridge in that county is given a number as it was discovered or built. Zane's Ranch was the fifth bridge discovered or built in the County of Humboldt, California and it therefore has the designation of 05-12-05. Sometimes you will see the first set of numbers replaced by the abbreviation for the state, thus CA-12-05.

A bridge is sometimes substantially rebuilt or replaced and it then has the suffix #2 added to it.

National Register of Historic Places: If the bridge has registered, the date is given.

Photographing Covered Bridges

Some standard positions
Portal: Taken to show the ends of bridge or bridge opening. This view, usually symmetrical, will include various signs posted. This is also a good way to get run over, so be careful!

3/4 view: Shows both the front and sides of the bridge, and is often the most attractive.

Side view: Taken from a bank or from the river, this gives not only a nice view of the bridge but usually allows for some interesting foreground elements.

Interior view: An image taken from the interior of the bridge will show some interesting structure but there is not a lot of available light. A tripod is important and HDR processing is helpful.

Landscape View: With the bridge smaller in the frame, you can introduce the habitat around it, particularly effective with colorful autumn foliage.

Using HDR(High Dynamic Range)

HDR is a process where multiple images of varying exposure are combined to make one image.

It has a bad name with some people because many HDR images are super-saturated, a kind of digital age version of an Elvis painted on velvet. However, the process is actually about getting a full range of exposure with no burnt out highlights or blocked shadows. This is an ideal processing solution for photographing Covered Bridges where you often have open light sky set against dark shadowed landscape and structure.

I use a series of three exposures at levels of -1 2/3, 0, +1 2/3, and this normally runs the full exposure range encountered. It is important to use a stable tripod.

One situation where you may need a larger series is shooting from within a bridge and using the window to frame an outside scene. The dynamic range is huge and you will need to have a series with a much larger range.

There are a number of software programs you can use to combine these images including newer editions of Photoshop. I use Photomatix which I have found very versatile and easy to use.

Best times for photographing bridges

Mornings and evenings are generally the best times for outdoor photography but the use of HDR processing makes it easier even in bright direct light. Although any season is good for bridge photography including the winter, fall foliage included in a scene can be spectacular.

A short history of Covered Bridges

Let's deal with that often posed question; "Why were the bridges covered"

1. Crossing animals thought it was a barn and entered easily. I like this suggestion, it shows imagination. However, its not the answer although the original bridges normally had no windows and this is said to be because animals would not be spooked by the sight of the water.

2. To cover up the unsightly truss structure. I don't think those early pioneers were that sensitive, and personally, I like the look of the trusses.

3. To keep snow off the traveled portion. In fact the bridge owners often paid to have the insides "snowed" in order to facilitate sleighs.

4. It offered some privacy to courting couples, hence "kissing bridges". That is a nice romantic notion but no.

In fact, the bridge was covered for economic reasons. The truss system was where much of the bridge's cost was found, and if left open to the elements, it deteriorated and the bridge became unstable and unsafe. Covering it protected this valuable portion and the roof could be replaced as needed with inexpensive materials and unskilled labor. Without coverings, a bridge might only have a life span of a decade while one that was covered often lasted 75 years or more before repairs became necessary. Besides extending the longevity of a bridge, wooden covered bridges had the virtue that they could be constructed of local materials and there were many available workers skilled in working with wood.

The first known Covered Bridge in North America was built in 1804 by Theodore Burr. It was called the Waterford bridge and it spanned the Hudson River in New York.

For the rest of the century and into the 20th Century, Covered bridge building boomed as the country became populated and people needed to travel between communities. The cost of constructing and maintaining a bridge was normally borne by the nearby community and many bridges charged a toll as a method of offsetting these costs.
The period from 1825 to 1875 was the heyday of bridge building but near the end of that period iron bridges began to supplant them.

The number of Covered bridges may have numbered 10,000 but have now dropped to about 950 spread throughout North America. Many have Historical Designations which provides them protection and many communities are interested in protecting their local historical bridges.

Glossary

Abutment: The abutments are the bridge supports on each side bank. Usually they were originally constructed of stone but they have often been replaced or supplemented with concrete through the years.

Arch: A curved timber or timber set which is shaped in a curve and functions as a support of the bridge.

Bed timbers: Timbers between the abutment and the truss or bottom chord.

Brace or bracing: A diagonal timber or timber set used to support the trusses.

Bridge Deck: The roadway through the bridge.

Buttress: Wood or metal members on the exterior sides which connect the floor beams and the top of the truss. Used to keep the bridge structure from twisting under wind, water and snow loads.

Camber: A planned curve in the structure to compensate for the weight of the structure.

Chord: The horizontal members extending the length of the truss meant to carry the load to the abutments.

Dead load: The load of the weight of the bridge itself.

Deck: The pathway through the bridge used by pedestrians or vehicles.

Pier: Stone/concrete supports built in the stream bed to support the bridge

Portal: The bridge's entrances.

Post: The truss's vertical members.

Span: The bridge length measured between the abutments.

Treenails or trunnels: Pins or dowels turned from hardwood, driven into holes drilled into the members of the truss to hold them together. Also used in mortised joints.

Truss: The framework which carries the load of the bridge and distributes it to the abutments.

Truss Types

A Truss is a system of ties and struts which are connected to act like a single beam to distribute and carry a load. In covered bridges, these Trusses carry the load to stone abutments at each side and perhaps piers in between. Following are the most common types of Trusses used in Covered Bridges.

Kingpost

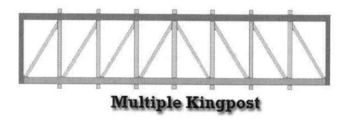

Multiple Kingpost

Kingpost is the simplest form of Truss with two diagonal members on a bottom chord, often with a vertical post connecting to the diagonals.
The multiple Kingpost involves a series of Kingposts symmetrical from the bridges center. This allows for a much longer span.

Queenpost

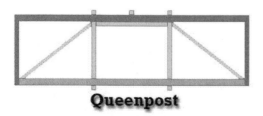

Queenpost

The Queenpost has the peak of the kingpost type replaced with a horizontal top chord which allows for a longer span.

Long

Long

The Long Truss was patented by Stephen Long in 1830. It is a series of X shaped diagonals connected to vertical posts.

Burr Arch

Burr Arch

Invented in 1804 by Theodore Burr, the Burr Arch is one of the most commonly found structures in Covered Bridge design. It is often used in combination with multiple kingposts. The ends of the arch are buried in the abutments.

Howe

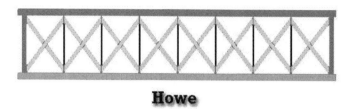

Howe

The Howe Truss was patented in 1840 by William Howe. It involves the use of vertical metal rods between the joints of wooden diagonals.

Town

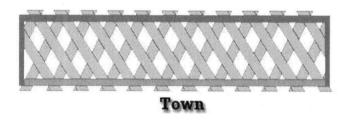

Town

The Town or lattice system was patented by Ithiel Town in 1820. It involved a system of overlapping diagonals in a lattice pattern connected at the intersection by Tree nails or trunnels, wooden pegs or dowels. It had the advantages in that it could be constructed by unskilled labor and local materials could be used.

Childs

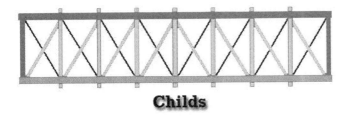

Childs

The Childs Truss System is essentially a multiple kingpost with half of the diagonal timbers replaced with iron bars.

Pratt

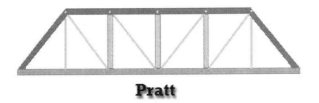

Pratt

The Pratt truss was patented in 1844 by Caleb Pratt and his son Thomas Willis Pratt. The design uses vertical members for compression and horizontal members to respond to tension.

Smith

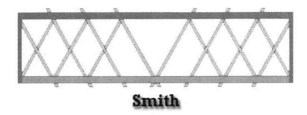

Smith

Robert W. Smith received patents in 1867 and 1869 for variations of his system.

Partridge

Partridge

Reuben L. Partridge received a patent for a design similar to the Smith system but adding terminal braces at the end and a central vertical member.

Warren

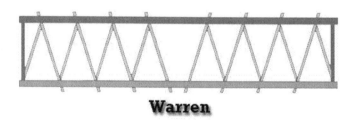

Warren

Patented in 1848 by two Englishmen, one of whom was named James Warren, it consists of parallel upper and lower chords with diagonal connecting members forming a series of equilateral triangles.

Paddleford

Paddleford

Peter Paddleford worked with the Long Truss system and eventually adapted it with a system of interlocking braces. he was never able to patent the system due to challenges from the owners of the Long Truss patent. However there are a number of New Hampshire and Vermont bridges which use the Paddleford system

Brown

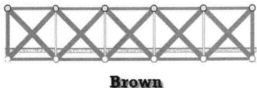

Brown

Josiah Brown Jr., of Buffalo, New York, patented this system in 1857.It consists of diagonal cross compression members connected to horizontal top and bottom stringers and is known for economic use of materials. It was only used in Michigan where there are a couple of surviving members.

Map of Virginia

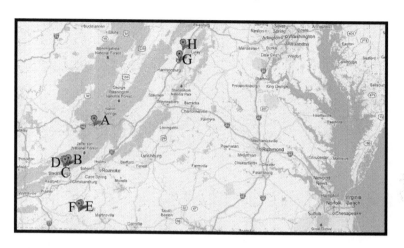

A. Humpback Covered Bridge
B. C.K. Reynolds Covered Bridge
C. Sinking Creek Covered Bridge
D. Link's Farm Covered Bridge
E. Bob White (Lower) Covered Bridge
F. Jack's Creek (Upper) Covered Bridge
G. Biedler Farm Covered Bridge
H. Meem's Bottom Covered Bridge

,pback Covered Bridge

Township: Covington
County: Alleghany

GPS Position: N 37° 48.017' W 80° 02.847'
Directions: From US-60 1.2 miles east of junction with I-64, go right on VA-600 for a short distance where you will see a park which is the site of the bridge.

Crosses: Dunlap Creek
Carries: Park road

Builder: Not known
Year Built: 1835 or 1857 (R1954)
Truss Type: Multiple Kingpost
Dimensions: 1 span, 100 feet

Photo Tip: Easy from all sides including good side views from creek level.

Notes: A unique bridge with the humpbacked appearance from building the center 4 feet higher than the portals. This may have been meant to prevent damage from floods. It was closed in 1924 and stood derelict until it was restored in 1954 through the efforts of local organizations and now is a popular exhibit. The "World Guide to Covered Bridges" lists it as having been built in 1835 but most other sources list it as 1857 and suggest the 1835 date is related to an earlier uncovered bridge.

World Index Number: 46-03-01

National Register of Historic Places: 10/01/1969

Sinking Creek Covered Bridge

Township: Newport
County: Giles

GPS Position: N 37° 18.403' W 80° 29.875'
Directions: From the town of Blacksburg go north on US-460and after 4.9 miles turn right on VA-42 and then after 1.0 miles turn left on VA-601. You will see the bridge on a bypassed section in about 0.7 miles.

Crosses: Sinking Creek
Carries: VA-601 (Bypassed Section)

Builder: Not known
Year Built: 1916 (R2000)
Truss Type: Queenpost
Dimensions: 1 Span, 70 feet

Photo Tip: Easy from all sides, and the memorial paving stones and flag offer nice elements to include.

Notes: When the bridge was bypassed by a concrete bridge in 1963, it was left in place but it wasn't until 1995 that the county of Giles claimed ownership. There are paving stones near the portal which record the names of contributors to the 2000 restoration. It is not in the National Register of Historic Places although it is likely eligible.

World Index Number: 46-35-01

National Register of Historic Places: Not registered

Link's Farm Covered Bridge

Township: Newport
County: Giles

GPS Position: N 37° 18.641' W 80° 30.996'
Directions: From the town of Newport go north on US-460 for 1.6 miles and turn right on VI-700. After 0.2 miles you will make a slight left on Covered Bridge Lane where you will see the bridge.

Crosses: Sinking Creek
Carries: VA-700 (Bypassed Section)

Builder: Not known
Year Built: 1912 (R1995)
Truss Type: Queenpost
Dimensions: 1 Span, 49 feet

Photo Tip: While it is on private property, it is easy to photograph from the road.

Notes: The bridge is on private property and is still in use by the owner. You need to obtain permission to visit it.

World Index Number: 46-35-02

National Register of Historic Places: Not registered

C.K. Reynolds Covered Bridge
(Red Maple Covered Bridge)

Township: Newport
County: Giles

GPS Position: N 37° 19.280' W 80° 27.027'
Directions: From Us-460 it is 3.5 miles northwest on VA-42 and then 0.3 miles on foot on a private road.

Crosses: Sinking Creek
Carries: Private lane

Builder: Harvey Black
Year Built: 1919 (R1980) (R1988)
Truss Type: Queenpost
Dimensions: 1 Span, 36 feet

Photo Tip: Easy from all sides bhut permission is needed

Notes: The bridge is on private property and you need to obtain permission to visit it.

World Index Number: 46-35-03

National Register of Historic Places: Not registered

Bob White Covered Bridge
(Lower Covered Bridge)

Township: Woolwine
County: Patrick

GPS Position: N 36° 46.805' W 80° 14.853'
Directions: From the town of Woolwine go southeast on VA-8 for 1.3 miles and turn left on State Route 618/Elamsville Rd and you will see bridge on a bypassed section in 1.1 miles.

Crosses: Smith River
Carries: Va-618 (Bypassed section)

Builder: Walter G. Weaver
Year Built: 1921
Truss Type: Queenpost
Dimensions: 2 Span, 80 feet

Photo Tip: Easy from all sides including the interior with covered trusses.

Notes: The bridge was named for the nearby post office, which was in turn named for the may Bobwhite Quail common in the area. It was bypassed in 1981. Patrick County has a bridge festival every June which includes activities at this bridge. The interior has diagonal wood sheaths which covers the truss.

World Index Number: 46-68-01

National Register of Historic Places: 5/22/1973

Jack's Creek Covered Bridge
(Upper Covered Bridge)

Township: Woolwine
County: Patrick

GPS Position: N 36° 45.868' W 80° 16.423'
Directions: From the town of Woolwine go south on VA-8 for 2.2 miles and turn right on State Route 615/Miles Rd and you will see bridge on a bypassed section in 0.2 miles.

Crosses: Smith River
Carries: Va-615 (Bypassed section)

Builder: Charles Vaughan
Year Built: 1916 (R1969) (R1974)
Truss Type: Queenpost
Dimensions: 1 Span, 48 feet

Photo Tip: Easy from all sides including the interior with covered trusses.

Notes: The bridge was named for the nearby Jack's Creek primitive Baptist Church which it was built to provide access. Patrick County has a bridge festival every June which includes activities at this bridge. The interior has diagonal wood sheaths which covers the truss. It was bypassed in 1932.

World Index Number: 46-68-02

National Register of Historic Places: 5/22/1973

Biedler Farm Covered Bridge

Township: Plains
County: Rockingham

GPS Position: N 38° 35.005' W 78° 42.666'
Directions: From I-81 Exit 264 it is northeast for 2.4 miles and then 0.5 miles on a private road.
Crosses: Smith Creek
Carries: Private lane

Builder: Daniel Ulrich Biedler
Year Built: 1896 (R1989)
Truss Type: Burr arch
Dimensions: 1 Span, 92 feet

Notes: The bridge is on private property and you need to obtain permission to visit it.

World Index Number: 46-79-01

National Register of Historic Places: Not registered

Meem's Bottom Covered Bridge

Township: Mount Jackson
County: Shenandoah

GPS Position: N 38° 43.238' W 78° 39.254'
Directions: From I-81 take exit 269 east on Caverns Rd/State Route 730 for 0.8 miles and turn left on US-11/Old Valley Pike. In 0.9 miles go left on State Road 70/Wissler Road where bridge is a short distance.

Crosses: North Fork of the Shenandoah River
Carries: **State Road** 70/Wissler Road

Builder: John W. B. Woods
Year Built: 1894 (R1979)
Truss Type: Multiple Kingpost and Burr arch
Dimensions: 4 spans including 3 added concrete piers, 203 feet

Photo Tip: Great side views, you might want to consider a panorama.

Notes: This bridge was burned by vandals 1976 and was salvaged and restored in 1979. In 1983 after a floor beam broke it was repaired and the piers as well as steel i-beams were added. It still carries traffic.

World Index Number: 46-82-01

National Register of Historic Places: 6/10/1975

Map of West Virginia

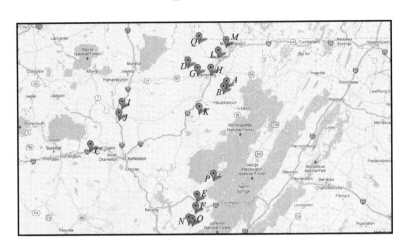

A. Philippi Covered Bridge
B. Carrollton Covered Bridge
C. Milton Covered Bridge
D. Center Point Covered Bridge
E. Herns Mill Covered Bridge
F. Hokes Mill Covered Bridge
G. Fletcher Covered Bridge
H. Simpson Creek Covered Bridge
I. Sarvis Fork Covered Bridge
J. Staats Mill Covered Bridge
K. Old Red Covered Bridge
L. Barrackville Covered Bridge
M. Dents Run Covered Bridge
N. Laurel Creek Covered Bridge
O. Indian Creek Covered Bridge
P. Denmar Covered Bridge
Q. Fish Creek Covered Bridge

Phillippi Covered Bridge

Township: Phillippi
County: Barbour

GPS Position: N 39° 09.217 W 80° 02.561'
Directions: In the town of Phillippi, it is on US-50 just east of the intersection of US-119

Crosses: Tygart Valley River
Carries: US-250

Builder: Lemuel Chenoweth
Year Built: 1852 (R1934) (R1991)
Truss Type: Burr Variation
Dimensions: 4 Spans (2 Piers have been added), 304 feet

Photo Tip: There are excellent viewpoints along the banks on both sides at the west side.

Notes: This is a magnificent structure with two active lanes of traffic (double-barreled) and a pedestrian walkway. It was used by both the North and South during the Civil War but thankfully neither side burnt it, as was the fate of many other bridges in that period. The 1934 repair brought it up to modern traffic standards.

World Index Number: 48-01-01

National Register of Historic Places: 09/14/1972

Carrollton Covered Bridge

Township: **Union**
County: Barbour

GPS Position: N 39° 05.423' W 80° 05.220'
Directions: From the town of Phillippi go south on US-119 for 5.0 km and turn left on Carrolton Road/ CR-36 where you will find the bridge in 0.7 miles.

Crosses: Buckhannon River
Carries: Carrolton Road/ CR-36

Builder: Daniel and Emmett J. O'Brien
Year Built: 1856 (R1962) (R2002)
Truss Type: Burr arch
Dimensions: 1 Span (+2 concrete piers added), 156 feet

Photo Tip: Easy from all sides including a good side view from the bank of the river.

Notes: This bridge still carries traffic and is in beautiful shape after the 2002 rehabilitation. In 1962 steel i-beams and two concrete piers were added to strengthen the structure.

World Index Number: 48-01-02

National Register of Historic Places: 06/04/1981

Milton Covered Bridge
(Sink's Mill, Mud River Covered Bridge)

Township: Milton
County: Cabell

GPS Position: N 38° 25.717' W 82° 07.972'
Directions: In the town of Milton take Pumpkin Way north off CR-16 and you will see the bridge on the park grounds

Crosses: Pond
Carries: none

Builder: R. H. Baker
Year Built: 1876 (R1971) (M2003)
Truss Type: Howe and Arch
Dimensions: 1 Span, 114 feet

Photo Tip: Easy from all sides and a nice reflection on the pond.

Notes: The bridge originally spanned the Mud River but was disassembled in 1977 and remained that way until it was re-assembled at its present site in 2003.

World Index Number: 48-06-01

National Register of Historic Places: 06/10/1975

Center Point Covered Bridge

Township: Center Point
County: Doddridge

GPS Position: N 39° 23.384' W 80° 38.051'
Directions: From the town of Wallace go west on Rinehart-Little Tenmile and continue on Pike Fork and you will see the bridge in 9.4 miles.

Crosses: Pike Fork of McElroy Creek
Carries: Pike Fork Road (Bypassed Section)

Builder: (Carpenters) John Ash and S.H. Smith, (Masons) T.C. Ancell and E. Underwood
Year Built: 1890 (R1982)
Truss Type: Long
Dimensions: 1 Span, 43 feet

Photo Tip: Easy from all sides including a nice side view.

Notes: The bridge carried public traffic until 1940 when it became privately owned. In 1981 it was donated to the Doddridge County Historical Society. In 1982 it was restored by volunteers.

World Index Number: 48-09-01

National Register of Historic Places: 08/29/1983

Hern's Mill Covered Bridge
(Milligan Creek Covered Bridge)

Township: Lewisburg
County: Greenbrier

GPS Position: N 37° 49.951' W 80° 30.263'
Directions: From the town of Lewisberg, go west on Midland Trail and after 2.4 miles turn left on CR-60/11 and after another 0.2 miles go left on CR-40/Hern's Mill Rd where you will find the bridge in 0.8 miles.

Crosses: Milligan's Creek
Carries: Hern's Mill Rd

Builder: Not known
Year Built: 1884 (R2000)
Truss Type: Queenpost
Dimensions: 1 Span, 54 feet

Photo Tip: There is a good side view which can be accessed from the northeast corner.
Notes: Concrete abutment caps and I-beam stringers were added in the rebuild in 2000. The narrow bridge still carries vehicle traffic. The bridge was originally built to provide access to the Hern's Mill as well as homeowners.

World Index Number: 48-13-01

National Register of Historic Places: 06/04/1981

Hoke's Mill Covered Bridge
(Second Creek Covered bridge)

Township: Irish Corner
County: Greenbrier

GPS Position: N 37° 41.871' W 80° 31.517'
Directions: From the town of Ronceverte go southeast on CR-48/River Road from US-19 and continue on CR-62/Hoke's Mill Rd and after 5.1 miles you will reach the bridge.

Crosses: Second Creek
Carries: Hoke's Mill Rd (Bypassed Section)

Builder: B.F. Mann, R.A. McDowell and Austin B. Erwin
Year Built: 1899 (R2001)
Truss Type: Long
Dimensions: 1 Span,82 feet

Photo Tip: Easy from all sides and a gorgeous creek bank side view.

Notes: Built to access the Hoke's Mill, it was closed to traffic in 1991. It looks great after a 2001 restoration

World Index Number: 48-13-02

National Register of Historic Places: 06/04/1981

Fletcher Covered Bridge
(Ten Mile Creek Covered Bridge)

Township: Ten Mile
County: Harrison

GPS Position: N 39° 18.319' W 80° 28.823'
Directions: From the village of Wolf Summit go west on
US-50 for 1.7 miles and turn right on Cr-5/Marshville Rd
and after 1.6 miles you will see the bridge on CR-5/29

Crosses: Ten Mile Creek
Carries: CR-5

Builder: Soloman Swiger (Abutments) L.E. Sturm
Year Built: 1891 (R2002)
Truss Type: Multiple Kingpost
Dimensions: 1 Span, 62 feet

Photo Tip: There is an excellent side view on the east side.

Notes: Named after a nearby family, the bridge is still in use. The original tin roof was replaced in the 2002 rebuild.

World Index Number: 48-17-03

National Register of Historic Places: 06/04/1981

Simpson Creek Covered Bridge
(Holland's Mill, W.T. Law Covered Bridge)

Township: Simpson
County: Harrison

GPS Position: N 39° 18.499' W 80° 16.763'
Directions: In the town of Bridgeport take exit 121 off I-91 onto Meadowbrook Road east and shortly turn left onto CR-24/2 where you will see the bridge on a bypassed section.

Crosses: Simpson Creek
Carries: CR-24/2 (Bypassed section)

Builder: Asa Hugill
Year Built: 1881 (M1888) (R2002)
Truss Type: Multiple Kingpost
Dimensions: 1 Span, 79 feet

Photo Tip: Easy from all sides in a quiet setting

Notes: The bridge was originally located a half a mile upstream and after being washed off its abutments by a 1888 flood, it was situated at its present location. The 2002 rebuild has it looking great

World Index Number: 48-17-12

National Register of Historic Places: 06/04/1981

Sarvis Fork Covered Bridge
(New Era, Sandy Creek Covered Bridge)

Township: Ravenswood
County: Jackson

GPS Position: N 38° 55.294' W 81° 38.697'
Directions: From the town of Sandyville go northeast on Parkersburg Road from Cr-21 for 1.3 miles and turn right on Sarvis Fork Road where you will find the bridge.

Crosses: Left Fork of Sandy Creek
Carries: Sarvis Fork Road

Builder: George W. Staats (Original bridge)
Year Built: 2000 (Replacement of a 1889 bridge)
Truss Type: Long and arch
Dimensions: 1 Span, 102 feet

Photo Tip: Excellent views from all sides including 3/4 and side view.

Notes: The original 1889 bridge was located near Angerona, West Virginia and it was moved to the present site in 1924. In 2000 the present bridge was built to replace it

World Index Number: 48-18-01#2

National Register of Historic Places: 06/04/1981 (Original bridge)

Staat's Mill Covered Bridge

Township: Washington
County: Jackson

GPS Position: N 38° 47.660' W 81° 41.212'
Directions: In the town of Ripley at the south end, enter the
Cedar Lakes Conference Center off Old US-21/ Cefar Lake

Crosses: Pond
Carries: None

Builder: H.T. Hartley
Year Built: 1886 (M1983)
Truss Type: Long
Dimensions: 1 Span, 101 feet

Photo Tip: Easy from all sides.

Notes: The bridge was originally three miles from the present site at the Tug Fork of the Bog Mill Creek and was named for Enoch Staat's mill. It was reconstructed on the present site in 1983.

World Index Number: 48-18-04

National Register of Historic Places: 05/29/1979

Old Red Covered Bridge
(Walkersville Covered Bridge)

Township: Settlement
County: Lewis

GPS Position: N 38° 51.511' W 80° 27.615'
Directions: Found just south of Walkersville, take US-19 about 1.0 mile and turn right on Big Gun Road where you will see the bridge.

Crosses: Right Fork of West Fork River
Carries: Big Gun Road

Builder: John G. Sprigg
Year Built: 1902 (R1963) (R2003)
Truss Type: Queenpost
Dimensions: 1 Span, 38 feet

Photo Tip: Easy from all sides.

Notes: A small but beautiful bridge found in a quiet setting

World Index Number: 48-21-03

National Register of Historic Places: 06/04/1981

Barracksville Covered Bridge

Township: Fairmont
County: Marion

GPS Position: N 39° 30.340' W 80° 10.077'
Directions: Found at the north end of the town of Barracksville on a bypassed section of CR-250 at the intersection of Pike St.

Crosses: Buffalo Creek
Carries: CR-250 (Bypassed section)

Builder: Eli and Lemuel Chenoweth
Year Built: 1853 (R1934) (R1951) (R2000)
Truss Type: Multiple Kingpost and Burr arch
Dimensions: 1 span, 145 feet

Photo Tip: Tight quarters make the side view difficult but think about a multiple shot panorama.

Notes: The bridge looks excellent after the 2000 work. The bridge was saved from destruction by Confederate soldiers when the local Ice family gave them food in exchange for it's safety.

World Index Number: 48-25-02

National **Register** of **Historic** Places: 03/30/1973

Dent's Run Covered Bridge
(Laurel Point Covered Bridge)

Township: Grant
County: Monongalia

GPS Position: N 39° 37.432' W 80° 02.452'
Directions: Found west of the town of Morgantown, go west on US-19 for 2.6 miles and turn right on Sugar Grove Road. After 0.6 miles turn left on CR-43/John Fox Road where you will find the bridge on a bypassed section in 0.2 miles.

Crosses: Dent's Run
Carries: CR-43 (Bypassed section)

Builder: William and Joseph Mercer, (Abutments) W.Y. Loar
Year Built: 1889 (R1984)
Truss Type: Kingpost
Dimensions: 1 span, 40 feet

Photo Tip: Easy from all sides, there is a good side view from across the highway.

Notes: Found in a quiet setting, this small bridge is in excellent shape.

World Index Number: 48-31-03

National Register of Historic Places: 06/04/1981

Laurel Creek Covered Bridge
(Lilydale, Arnott Covered Bridge)

Township: Springfield
County: Monroe

GPS Position: N 37° 33.680' W 80° 37.573'
Directions: From the town of Union go southeast on US-219/Koontz Rd for 2.7 miles and turn right on CR-219/7. In 2.7 miles make a slight right on Cr-23/Laurel Creek Road and then after 2.8 miles turn left on CR-219/Laurel Creek Road where you will find the bridge in 0.9 miles.

Crosses: Laurel Creek
Carries: Laurel Creek Road

Builder: Charles Robert Arnott, (Abutments) Lewis Miller
Year Built: 1911 (R200)
Truss Type: Queenpost
Dimensions: 1 Span, 25 feet

Photo Tip: Good from all sides including a good creek level side view from the west.

Notes: At 25 feet, this is West Virginia's shortest bridge. It looks to be in great shape.

World Index Number: 48-32-01

National Register of Historic Places: 06/04/1981

Indian Creek Covered Bridge
(Salt Sulphur Springs Covered Bridge)

Township: Springfield
County: Monroe

GPS Position: N 37° 32.814' W 80° 34.498'
Directions: From the town of Union go southwest on South
St and continue on US-219/Koontz Rd where you will find
the bridge after 4.4 miles.

Crosses: Indian Creek
Carries: US-219 (Bypassed section)

Builder: Oscar and Ray Weikel
Year Built: 1903 (R1965) (R2000)
Truss Type: Long
Dimensions: 1 Span, 51 feet

Photo Tip: Easy from all sides and an interesting interior as
well.

Notes: A great looking bridge with its chocolate colored sides set off by the trees behind it. The builders were 16 and 18 years old at the time of construction.

World Index Number: 48-32-02

National Register of Historic Places: 04/01/1975

Denmar Covered Bridge
(Locust Creek Covered Bridge)

Township: Little Levels
County: Pocahontas

GPS Position: N 38° 04.754' W 80° 14.992'
Directions: from the town of Hillsboro go west on US-219 for 1.8 miles and turn left on Locust Creek Road and then after 3.1 miles turn right on CR-31/Denmar Road where you will see the bridge.

Crosses: Locust Creek
Carries: CR-31/Denmar Road (Bypassed section)

Builder: R.N. Bruce
Year Built: 1888 (R1904) (R2004)
Truss Type: Smith
Dimensions: 1 Span, 118 feet

Photo Tip: Excellent all sides including a side view from the new bridge.

Notes: There are no windows in this great looking brown sided bridge.

World Index Number: 48-38-01

National Register of Historic Places: 06/04/1981

Hundred Covered Bridge
(Fish Creek Covered Bridge)

Township: Hundred
County: Wetzel

GPS Position: N 39° 40.363' W 80° 27.122'
Directions: From the east side of the village of Hundred take CR-1/3 south from US-250 and you will see the bridge.

Crosses: Fish Creek
Carries: CR-1/3

Builder: Family of C.W. Critchfield (Original bridge)
Year Built: 2001 (Replaced the original bridge from 1881)
Truss Type: Kingpost
Dimensions: 1 Span, 36 feet

Photo Tip: Easy 3/4 and side views.

Notes: The rebuilt bridge used 4 timber braces from the old bridge but was otherwise built with new material and used steel stringers along with the kingpost trusses.

World Index Number: 48-52-01#2

National Register of Historic Places: 06/04/1981
(Original bridge)

The Photographer's and Explorer's Series by Harold Stiver

1. New York Covered Bridges

2. Ontario's Old Mills

3. Massachusetts Covered Bridges

4. Michigan Covered Bridges

5. Connecticut Covered Bridges

6. Vermont Covered Bridges

7. Indiana Covered Bridges

8. New England Covered Bridges

9. Maine Covered Bridges

10. Birding Guide to Orkney

11. New Hampshire Covered Bridges

12. Kentucky Covered Bridges

13. Tennessee Covered Bridges

14. West Virginia Covered Bridges

Index

31212137R00044

Made in the USA
Lexington, KY
02 April 2014